Poems & Coloring Book

Copyright © 2023 by Franklyn James

All rights reserved. No part of this publication may be reproduced, distributed, or transmitted in any form or by any means, including photocopying, recording, or other electronic or mechanical methods, without the prior written permission of the author/publisher, except as permitted by copyright law.

For permissions, inquiries, or collaboration: https://linktr.ee/franklyn3i

Written by Franklyn James

First Edition

ISBN (Paperback): 979-8-8735820-6-8
ISBN (Hardcover): 979-8-9853434-9-6

# The Little Things We Take for Granted

**Poems & Coloring Book**

*Written by* **Franklyn James**

## Dedication

To every curious child who marvels at the sky,
to those who laugh out loud and aren't afraid to cry.
This book is dedicated to you who find delight,
in the little things each day, from morning 'til night.

# Welcome to The Little Things We Take for Granted!

Hi, little friends! Do you know what's special about you? It's not just your name or how you look. It's also the small things you do every day. Like a quick hiccup, a laugh, or your smiling face. These little things are super special!

Sometimes, these little things, like a big burp or a funny toot, can be loud. They might make us giggle, but remember to be nice and polite.

This book is full of pictures to color. Each page has a cute drawing and a funny little poem about these little things. You can make them bright with your favorite colors!

Reading Together

Read the poems with your mom, dad, brother, sister, or family member. They can read to you while you make each page beautiful with colors. It's fun to read, laugh, and color together.

In a cozy room, little feet wiggle,
a book in hand, we both giggle.
Mom reads aloud, in voices so funny
Pictures come alive—is that a bunny?

I color the pages with reds, greens, and purples,
making magic scenes from the lines and circles.
Together we read, laugh, and play,
In our coloring book, every single day.

There's no wrong way to color. Use your brightest colors, mix them, or even add sparkles! Each page allows you to show your creativity and enjoy the small things we sometimes don't notice.

Grab your crayons or markers, let's color, and have fun!

Happy Coloring!

## Smile

A sunny smile, wide and bright,

turns the day from dark to light.

Share your joy, spread it wide,

in every smile, love resides.

## Hiccups

A hiccup comes, a funny jump,
inside your tummy, a little bump.
Laugh it out, your eyes light up.
With each hiccup, Say "giddy-up!"

## Toot

A little toot, isn't it cute?

Like a trumpet in a suit.

Giggle and play, it's okay,

soon the smell will go away.

## Burp

After eating, comes a burp,

soft and gentle, not a chirp.

Excuse yourself, smile real wide;

it's so natural, no need to hide.

## Cry

Tears fall down, when we're sad, it's true,

let them go, they're a part of you.

After rain, the sun will shine,

you'll smile again, everything's fine.

**Pee**

To the bathroom, quick, let's race,

kindly pee and leave no trace.

Line up neat, it's your turn,

We wash our hands, bye-bye, germs!

## Cough

A little cough, a quick cover,
keep it safe, look after each other.
With clean hands, we play and beam,
together we're clean, a healthy team.

## Yawn

Yawning wide in morning's light,
welcoming the day so bright.
Stretch and yawn, embrace the new,
each day's a gift, fresh and true.

## Awake

Rubbing eyes, awake from a dream,

in my room lights softly stream.

Each day starts with sleepy eyes,

waking up to sunny skies.

## Poo

In the loo, something new,
everybody poos, it's true!
Flush away, wave goodbye,
clean and fresh, under the sky.

## Bonus Pages

Bonus friends, with stripes and tails,

their grins and charm never fail.

Extra pages to color with glee,

our pals are as happy as can be!

# Meet Mr. Franklyn James!

Mr. Franklyn grew up in sunny Jamaica, but now he lives in Canada. There, he loves to teach, talk about God, and create beautiful art. He believes that everything we learn and do is important because it helps us and others grow.

He writes books to share his ideas with everyone. One of his books, Tone of Transition, discusses how we can better understand each other when we talk and listen.

He also writes poems in a book called Shards of Longing, using words to paint pictures about feelings and dreams, even the ones we don't always say out loud.

Another book, The Body in Narrative, explains how characters in stories can show what they feel through their actions, such as when they're happy or surprised.

He's also made this fun book. The Little Things We Take for Granted is about the tiny, amazing things our bodies do, like sneezing or peeing!

And in Death: The Epithet of Excellence, Mr. Franklyn shows how Death can be an artist too; using stories, music, and memories to help us remember the people we love. Even when someone is gone, their love stays with us in poems, pictures, and the names we carry.

Mr. Franklyn likes to help people think about big ideas and feelings in a way that makes sense. He helps us see how special words can be and loves to use his stories and poems to help make the world a better place.

www.ingramcontent.com/pod-product-compliance
Lightning Source LLC
Chambersburg PA
CBHW080746060526
44119CB00072B/159